First US edition 2023
First published by Big Picture Press,
an imprint of Bonnier Books UK, 2022

Library of Congress Catalog Card Number 2022922829
ISBN 978-1-5362-3262-2

23 24 25 26 27 28 TLF 10 9 8 7 6 5 4 3 2 1

Printed in Dongguan, Guangdong, China

For Astrid —BT
For Otis and Tristan —CB

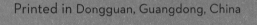

This book was typeset in
Core Circus Rough and Neutraface Text.
The illustrations were created digitally.

BIG PICTURE PRESS
an imprint of
Candlewick Press
99 Dover Street
Somerville, Massachusetts 02144

www.candlewick.com

MAMMALS

EVERYWHERE

ILLUSTRATED BY BRITTA TECKENTRUP
WRITTEN BY CAMILLA DE LA BEDOYERE

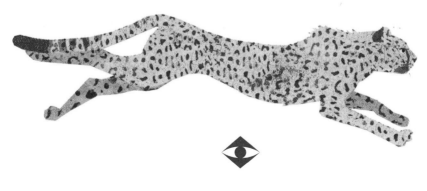

BPP

THERE ARE MAMMALS EVERYWHERE

Mammals live almost everywhere on earth, and they come in an astonishing array of shapes and sizes. Tiny **bumblebee bats**, fluttering through the forest, are smaller than your thumb. The colossal **blue whale** swims in the deep ocean and—at more than 98 feet/30 meters long—is the largest animal to ever live. But wherever they live and whatever their size, a characteristic that all mammals have in common is that they feed their young with milk.

Bumblebee bat

Masai giraffe

African elephant

African black rhinoceros

Plains zebra

Black panther

Common hippopotamus

Cheetah

Crested porcupine

Zorilla

Domestic cat

Some of these mammals are record-breakers! Which mammal do you think is the deadliest to humans? Can you also find the mammal with the best sense of smell, the fastest mammal over a long distance, and the mammal that can make a foul smell?

IT'S A MAMMAL!
(SO WHAT *IS* THAT?)

There are over 6,000 species of mammals alive today. Mammals may look very different from one another, but they all have bony **skeletons** that allow them to perform a wide range of movements. Some mammals have four legs and a tail, while others walk on two legs, fly using two wings, or move using flippers and fins.

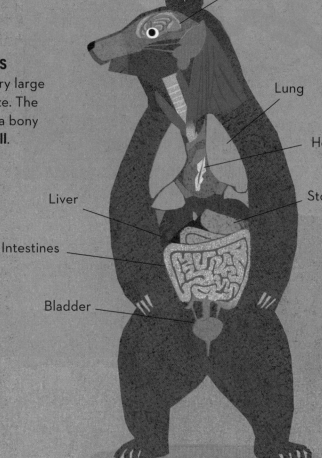

Brain

Lung

Heart

Stomach

Liver

Intestines

Bladder

BIG BRAINS

A mammal's brain is very large relative to its body size. The brain is protected by a bony case called a **skull**.

BREATHING AIR

All mammals use **lungs** to breathe air, even the mammals that live in water. Air moves through the nose or mouth until it reaches the lungs, where the **oxygen** is absorbed. The oxygen then passes into the **blood vessels** and the **heart**, which pumps the blood throughout the body.

RECORD-BREAKERS

Everyone knows that dogs have a superb sense of smell, but **polar bears** have record-breaking snouts. They have been known to catch the scent of a seal from 20 miles/ 32 kilometers away.

Black rats may not look deadly, but they are more dangerous to humans than any other mammal because they can spread disease, including food poisoning and plagues.

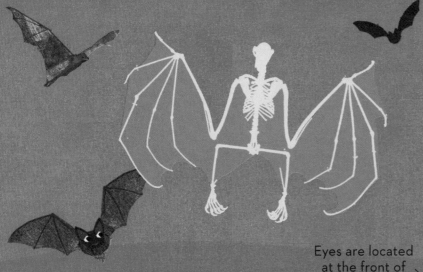

BATS

Bats are the only mammals that have wings and can fly. Each wing is made up of a large sheet of leathery skin that stretches from the long, skinny bones of the front limb down to the bat's leg. The largest bats are huge, with a wingspan of 5 feet/1.5 meters or more.

CATS

Members of the **cat** family have strong, flexible bodies that allow them to run, climb, and pounce. They have powerful legs and feet that are equipped with claws, and their jaws are lined with sharp teeth. Long tails help them balance as they quietly stalk their prey.

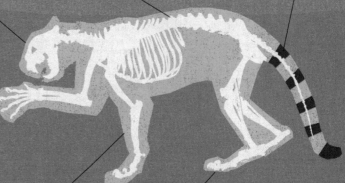

Fur may be colored with spots or stripes to provide **camouflage**.

Long, flexible spine

Eyes are located at the front of the face to focus on prey.

Large muscles for running

Claws for gripping on to the ground, tree bark, or prey

PINNIPEDS

Seals, **sea lions**, and **walruses** belong to a group of mammals called **pinnipeds**. They live in water and have flippers and strong tails for diving and swimming. Pinnipeds have a thick layer of fat, called **blubber**, beneath their skin to keep them warm in cold waters. Some have furry bodies, but others have smooth skin and whiskered snouts.

The fastest mammal over a long distance is actually the **pronghorn**. It can keep up a top speed of 35 miles/56 kilometers per hour before it needs a rest.

Many mammals make foul smells to scare other animals away, but a **zorilla** could probably outstink them all. It sprays a burning liquid from its bottom that smells so terrible even lions turn tail when they see a zorilla nearby!

MAMMALS HAVE BEEN AROUND FOR AGES

Morganucodon

Mammals have been around for a really long time. The first mammals looked like **shrews**, which are tiny mouselike animals with long, whiskered snouts. These early mammals lived about 210 million years ago, when **dinosaurs** walked the earth, and none of them grew much bigger than a cat! When the dinosaurs died out, mammals began to change and evolve into the vast range of creatures that live today.

210 MILLION YEARS AGO

Morganucodon was one of the earliest mammals. It was a small, furry creature that ate insects.

Elasmotherium

Gigantopithecus

Two million years ago, our human ancestors would have kept a safe distance from this giant rhinoceros! ***Elasmotherium*** was a plant-eater, but it was equipped with a huge, scary horn on its head.

Megatherium

The mighty ***Gigantopithecus*** was likely one of the tallest mammals to ever live—reaching an impressive 10 feet/3 meters in height. This giant ape lived in warm forests approximately 1 million years ago.

Megatherium grew an incredible 20 feet/6 meters long. This giant sloth lived 10,000 years ago and used its long claws to reach leaves high up in trees.

Eomaia

Sifrhippus

Eomaia lived 125 million years ago. It was a long-snouted mammal that grew to be 4 inches/10 centimeters long. Rather than laying eggs, *Eomaia* gave birth to their young, just as modern mammals do.

The first horses were the size of a cat and ate leaves instead of grass. **Sifrhippus** lived about 50 million years ago, when the world was much warmer than it is today.

Apidium

Pakicetus

Monkeys and apes evolved from animals such as **Apidium**, which lived 30 million years ago. *Apidium* jumped from branch to branch, eating fruit and flowers, just like many of its modern relatives.

About 50 million years ago, the first whales lived on land, not in the ocean! **Pakicetus** probably spent most of its time hunting on land, occasionally swimming in shallow water to look for fish to eat.

Woolly mammoth

Giraffe

Woolly mammoths had long, shaggy fur to keep them warm during the last ice age. They went extinct about 5,000 years ago when temperatures increased.

The tallest land animal today is the **giraffe**. It can grow to 18 feet/5.5 meters in height and uses its long neck to reach leaves high up in the trees.

WHAT MAKES MAMMALS UNIQUE?

Mammals are a large and very successful group of animals. They have been able to spread across the world and survive in all types of habitats because they have some impressive ways to stay warm, feed their young, and get food.

WARM BLOOD

Mammals are **warm-blooded**—which means they can regulate their body temperature. This allows them to stay warm even if their environment is cold. They can also cool themselves down when they get too hot— they often do this by sweating or panting. African elephants flap their huge ears to cool down!

BIG BRAINS

Many mammals are intelligent animals that can play, learn, and solve problems. This helps them develop the skills they need to stay safe from predators and find food.

HAIR

Hair, or fur, grows from a mammal's skin. It can be thick or sparse, but every mammal has it. Fur can keep mammals warm, and different colors and patterns of fur can help **camouflage** mammals so they can hide from predators or prey.

BABIES AND MILK

Almost all mammals give birth to their babies (rather than laying eggs). The mother feeds them with milk that is produced in a special part of her body called **mammary glands**. The milk is very nutritious for the babies, and it protects them from disease.

SEA OTTERS

Sea otters can be spotted floating in the Pacific Ocean. They are most abundant around kelp seabeds, where the world's largest and fastest-growing seaweed is found. The otters dive below the waves to find shellfish, fish, and crabs to eat.

Sea otters have between 600,000 to 1,000,000 hair follicles per square inch of their skin, or approximately 125,000 hair follicles per square centimeter of skin. The hairs are very fine, and air gets trapped between each strand. The hair and trapped air keeps the otter warm, like a thick, waterproof blanket. It also works like a life jacket, helping an otter float.

A sea otter mother gives birth to one baby at a time, called a **pup**. While she floats in the water, she rests the pup on her belly.

3. The sea otter floats on its back and rests the stone on its belly. It bashes the shellfish against the stone until it cracks open.

2. Some shellfish are very tough, so the otter also collects a stone from the seabed and swims to the surface with it.

1. A hungry sea otter uses its handlike paws to pick **sea urchins** off the **kelp** or grab shellfish, such as **clams**, from the seabed.

CAN YOU FIND IT?
Long-spined **sea urchins** eat giant kelp and can damage the sea otters' habitat. How many sea urchins can you spot grazing on the huge fronds of seaweed?

WHERE DO MAMMALS LIVE?

About 98% of all species of mammals live on land. However, there are groups of mammals that spend most, or all, of their lives in water. These include **pinnipeds**, **whales**, and **dolphins**. Other groups of mammals are superb swimmers and spend lots of time in the water, but they may give birth or raise their young on land.

WHALES

Whales are perfectly adapted to life in the ocean. They have smooth skin and torpedo-shaped bodies that slip easily through the water. They have **flippers** instead of legs, and they breathe using a blowhole at the top of their head.

Female whales give birth in the ocean. Their babies are called **calves**, and they stay close to their mother as they grow and learn how to find food.

Blue whale babies are enormous and grow a thousand times faster than a human baby!

BEAVERS

Beavers belong to a group of mammals called **rodents**, which have super-strong front teeth. They use these teeth to gnaw trees and branches. They then use the collected wood to build their homes in the middle of a pond or slow-flowing river.

A beaver's home is called a **lodge**. It contains rooms, called **chambers**, where young beavers are kept safe from predators.

Beavers are good swimmers. They enter the lodge through tunnels that are accessed underwater. Their home keeps them safe and warm during long, cold winters.

CAN YOU FIND IT?
Other animals, such as **water voles**, also camp out in beaver lodges. Can you find one of these small, furry rodents with a long tail?

TUNDRA

The land around the Arctic is called the **tundra**, and it is famous for its snowy blizzards and blustery winds. It is a difficult place to live—unless you can stay snug inside your own superthick fur coat. **Musk oxen** have hair that almost reaches their toes, and they snuggle up next to each other to benefit from some buddy-body-warmth!

FORESTS

Tropical forests are packed with tall trees that bloom all year round, producing plenty of fruit for any animals that can reach it. **Orangutans** spend almost all their lives in the treetops, using their strong arms to climb from tree to tree, searching for ripe fruit.

DESERTS

Deserts are very dry habitats that experience extreme temperatures. **Bactrian camels** survive desert life by storing fat inside their two **humps** that they can later convert into energy. They grow thick, shaggy fur for the icy winter and shed it for the hot summer months.

CAVES

Many species of bats gather together in caves in big groups called **colonies**. They rest during the day by hanging upside down from the cave ceiling and go hunting at night. Some caves can house more than five million bats!

THE SAVANNA

As the sun sets over the African grassland, mammals gather around a water hole to make the most of the cooler temperatures. This habitat is called the savanna, and it is home to many herds of grass-eating mammals, along with the **predators** that hunt them.

African black rhinoceroses appear bald, apart from some hairs sprouting on their heads and the tufts on their tails, which they use to swat flies away. These huge mammals like to cover themselves in mud—it cools them down and dries to a thick layer that protects their skin, like sunscreen!

Antelope look like deer, but they are more closely related to the bovines, such as cows. Antelope stomachs have four **chambers**, which help them digest tough grasses on the savanna.

One of the most peculiar mammals of the savanna is the **aardvark**. It is one of the fastest-burrowing animals in the world, and it is rarely seen except at nighttime, when it emerges from its den to feast on **ants** and **termites**.

CAN YOU FIND IT?
Giraffes are animals of the savanna, but when they are grazing on leaves they can blend in with the trees and be hard to see. Can you spot a giraffe's head poking up above some trees?

Long-legged pigs, called **warthogs**, run across the savanna, with a row of piglets trotting behind. Warthogs raise their young in burrows dug by other animals, such as **aardvarks**.

A group of **hyenas** is called a **clan** and it is led by a female. Hyenas are skillful hunters and may even attack large animals such as **elephants** and **water buffalo**.

A family of **lions** is called a **pride**. The female lions in the pride work as a team to hunt **antelope** and **zebras**, while the male lion protects the cubs, relaxing in the shade of an acacia tree.

Hippopotamuses love to wallow in the water during the hot daytime, but at night they emerge onto land to eat grass.

Small animals on the savanna need to be on the lookout for danger at all times. **Meerkats** stand on mounds to spy **snakes** and other predators and hide in underground burrows when they sense danger.

Zebras belong to the horse family. They live in large herds that feed together, keeping a watchful eye out for predators. Their striped fur can confuse predators when the herd gallops away.

STAYING ALIVE

Fur is a very useful skin covering. Not only does it keep a mammal warm and protect the soft skin beneath, but it can also come in all sorts of colors and patterns. These colors, stripes, blotches, and spots can be used to camouflage an animal, helping it hide from both **predators** and **prey**.

SHOW-OFFS

In snowy places, such as the Arctic and mountaintops, many mammals grow white fur to help them **camouflage** in the winter. In the summer, some of them grow brown or gray fur instead, which helps them hide among rocks and plants.

CAN YOU FIND IT?

There are six different species of mammals hiding in this arctic scene—can you find them all?

MASTERS OF SURVIVAL

SCALES

The soft body of a **Chinese pangolin** is protected by a layer of overlapping scales, like a suit of armor. Its belly and throat have no scales, but they are hidden when the pangolin rolls up into a ball, making it difficult to attack.

HORNS

African buffalo are big, powerful beasts. If a **lion** attacks a herd of buffalo, they form a circle around the youngest members of the herd and use their horns to defend themselves. A buffalo's mighty horns can easily stab and slash a lion's skin.

SPINES

The spines of a **porcupine** are actually sharp, stiff hairs, called **quills**. The North American porcupine has 300,000 quills, and each one has about 700 tiny **barbs** near its tip. The barbs grip into the flesh of an attacker, making it very painful to retreat!

BUILD A HOME

Tiny **harvest mice** make easy prey for **birds**, **snakes**, and other animals. They build nests from straw, raised above the ground where they can hide their babies from predators. The nest is the shape of a hollow ball, and it's attached to reeds or tall stalks of grass.

POISON

Before a **slow loris** leaves her baby to search for food, she licks them! Special parts of her elbows ooze a poison, which she licks and then spreads on her baby. It tastes toxic and smells bad, so predators think twice before attacking the youngster.

FEEDING

One of the reasons that mammals are such a successful group of animals is that they have developed some incredible ways to find and eat all sorts of food—from **ants** to **zebras**!

SENSES

Before an animal can eat, it has to find its food. Mammals have superb **senses**, such as sight, hearing, and smell that are perfect for seeking different sources of food.

When a **star-nosed mole** is on the hunt for **worms** or **snails** to eat, it wiggles the twenty-two soft, fleshy tentacles on its snout. The tentacles detect the smell and movement of other creatures.

A **tarsier**'s eyeballs are bigger than its brain! It hunts at night, and its big eyes detect as much light as possible in the dark rain forest.

Large ears are perfect for "catching" sound and directing it to a mammal's **eardrum**, where the sound is turned into signals that pass to the brain. **Fennec foxes** use their huge ears to listen for the sounds of potential prey moving beneath the sand.

As a **dolphin** swims, it makes clicking sounds. These sound waves travel through the water until they come across obstacles such as fish. The sound waves then bounce back to the dolphin and give it information about the size and position of the fish. This process is called **echolocation**, and it's one way for mammals to find food. **Bats** use it, too!

TEETH

Mammals that eat a meat-based diet are called **carnivores**, and their teeth are good at biting, tearing, and slicing. **Herbivores** are animals that eat plants, and their teeth are the perfect shape for snipping leaves and stems and grinding them into a mush that can be easily swallowed.

Tigers have long, daggerlike teeth for biting, called **fangs**, or **canine teeth**—they can be as long as an adult's finger! Tigers also have **carnassial teeth** on the side of their jaws that fit together like scissor blades to cut into meat.

Sheep eat mostly grass, and they use the small, sharp **incisors** at the front of their jaw to snip this tough plant. Large grinding teeth at the back of the mouth are called **molars**. They have ridges that help grind up the grass.

NO TEETH

Most mammals have teeth, but **giant anteaters**, **duck-billed platypuses**, and some **whales** are toothless.

Most **whales** have cone-shaped teeth for catching **fish** and **squid**, but **baleen whales** have sievelike sheets called **baleen plates**. When the whale gulps a mouthful of water, the baleen plates trap small creatures, such as **shrimp** and **krill**.

Giant anteaters use their superb sense of smell to sniff out ant nests and termite mounds. They rip these structures open with their long, curved claws and then scoop up the insects using a very long, sticky tongue. They can devour 35,000 bugs in one day!

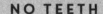

One of the world's strangest mammals is the **duck-billed platypus**. It has a beak-shaped snout that can sense the electrical signals given off by its prey in water.

MOVING

As dawn breaks above an Asian rain forest and early morning sunlight shines on the tall treetops, two distinctive sounds can be heard: singing and rustling. The **gibbons** are awake and on the move!

Gibbons are a type of **ape**. Gibbons are rightly known as the king of the swingers because these apes can race through the trees, swinging from branch to branch. Gibbons also leap long distances, traveling more than 33 feet/10 meters in a single jump.

CAN YOU FIND IT?
Gibbons make a move when there are predators about. Can you spot a hungry **black eagle** that is lurking in the jungle?

To travel through the jungle, gibbons use their hands to grip branches and swing their bodies to move through trees. This type of movement is called **brachiation**.

2. The gibbon's body swings around so the second arm can reach out.

1. Holding on tight to the branch with one hand, the gibbon swings its body forward.

3. The gibbon's hand grabs the next branch, and the first arm now reaches forward.

When gibbons want to talk to one another they sing songs that echo through the jungle. Their beautiful love duets—performed by a male and a female—sound like eerie whoops and wails.

4. When the gibbon is ready to stop, it uses a foot to grip a lower branch and steady its body.

RECORD-BREAKERS

The fastest runners over a short distance are **cheetahs**. They can achieve top speeds of 70 miles per hour/112 kilometers per hour when chasing **antelope**, but they can run for only about 60 seconds before they get too hot. A cheetah's long tail helps it balance as it turns corners, and it uses its claws to grip the ground, like the spikes on an athlete's running shoes.

Being springy is a surprisingly good way of moving at high speeds—and leaping out of danger! **Red kangaroos** can jump on average 25 feet/7.5 meters in a single bound, and they reach heights of 6 feet/2 meters.

MAMMAL PARENTS

Most mammal babies stay within the womb until they are fully developed with the exception of **monotremes**, which lay eggs, and **marsupials**, which raise their babies in pouches.

EGG-LAYING MAMMALS

There are just five species of mammals that lay eggs: four species of **echidna** and the **duck-billed platypus**.

Echidnas can grow up to 40 inches/ 100 centimeters long. They have short legs, a long snout, and tiny eyes, and they have spines growing between strands of hair. Some echidnas lay a single egg in a **burrow**, while others keep their egg in a **pouch**.

MAMMALS WITH POUCHES

There are about three hundred species of **marsupials**, and, like the **monotremes**, many of them live in or around Australia. **Koalas**, **kangaroos**, **quolls**, **wombats**, and **opossums** are all types of marsupials.

A kangaroo **joey** stays in its mother's pouch for several months as it grows, although it may climb out from time to time to stretch its legs!

Female kangaroos give birth to tiny babies, called **joeys**, which are often no bigger than a jelly bean. A joey must make its own way to the mother's **pouch**, where it latches on to a teat and suckles on its mother's milk.

PARENTING SKILLS: GRAY WOLVES

Gray wolves live in large family groups called **packs**. Every pack has a hierarchal order led by a breeding pair.

In spring, the breeding pair mate. The two wolves nuzzle each other, touching noses and grooming each other's fur. The wolves form a close bond that lasts for a lifetime.

At **seven months old**, the playful pups are allowed to join the pack on hunting trips. They watch the adults and learn how to find, chase, and kill prey.

The female is pregnant for about **sixty days**, and she uses this time to dig a **den** where she will raise her **pups**. She can expect four to six pups to be born in her litter.

When the pups are **four weeks old**, they are able to leave the den and explore. They now have teeth and can start to eat meat.

Pups are born blind and deaf, but they have a good sense of smell. The pups begin by drinking milk, but as they grow, adults in the pack provide regurgitated food for the pups to eat.

The whole pack helps care for the growing pups, and they even babysit when the breeding pair go hunting.

AFRICAN ELEPHANTS

In the hot desert lands of Mali, in Africa, **elephant** families set out on an epic journey each year in search of food and water. Only by working as a team and taking care of one another can these huge mammals survive in this harsh habitat.

At the beginning of the **dry season**, herds of elephants roam along marshes, just south of Timbuktu. There is water here, and some small trees grow along the edge of desert sands.

A baby elephant—a **calf**—lies in the mud to cool down. Calves are cared for by their mothers, aunts, cousins, and siblings. Adults will sometimes stroke the calf or gently tap it with their trunks if it moves too far from the safety of the herd.

There has been no rain for some time, so the land is dry and the plants are dying. It is time for the herd to move west. They start a journey that will cover about 300 miles/500 kilometers, much of it in blistering heat and sudden sandstorms.

When the rainy season is over, the elephants continue their circular route, back to where they began in the marshes of the north.

A female elephant, called the **matriarch**, leads the herd. She is oldest member of the herd and can remember the route they must take in the search for water. She scans the sky for signs of rain clouds.

The elephants reach Lake Banzena, where they rest, seeking shade in thickets of trees while they wait for the rainy season to begin. They talk to each other by making low rumbling sounds that travel long distances through the ground. Elephants "hear" the rumbles through their sensitive feet.

CAN YOU FIND IT?

Elephants produce lots of poop, or **dung**. **Dung beetles** collect the dung, roll it into a ball, and lay their eggs in it. When the eggs hatch, the **grubs** eat the dung. How many dung beetles can you find?

The gray clouds on the horizon tell the elephants that rains are falling in the south, and they begin the next stage of their trek. Their traditional route takes them through villages that have been built in the area, so now they must walk even farther to avoid the villagers.

Finally, the herd reaches the lush grasslands of Boni. The **rainy season** has turned the land green, with plants springing up everywhere. The water holes are full again, and the elephants can play together in the water, enjoying a well-earned rest.

The elephants have to travel quickly so they can reach the rains before dying of thirst or starvation. Young elephants are helped along by their family and allowed to rest in the shade of the elders' larger bodies.

MAMMALS AND PEOPLE

The lives of mammals have been intertwined with those of humans since the earliest times. For many thousands of years, people have hunted mammals for sustenance and used their skins and furs for clothing. **Cattle**, **camels**, **llamas**, and **horses** have been used to plow the land or carry people and their goods far across the globe.

PEOPLE AND PETS

Wild **cats** may have been tamed, or **domesticated**, more than 10,000 years ago! The first **dogs** lived among humans even earlier, when **wolves** were used on hunting trips during the last ice age. Today, cats and dogs are still much-loved companions.

MAMMALS AT WORK

Some mammals have been trained to do important tasks. **Assistance dogs** help people who cannot see or hear or who have difficulties with mobility. Life-saving **rats** have been trained to sniff out bombs in war zones, and **mice** have been taught to find dangerous drugs that pass through airports.

MYTHS AND LEGENDS

All over the world, people have put mammals at the center of their stories. These legends include flying **horses**, such as **Pegasus** from Greek myth. Some world religions revere mammals such as **cows**, **bears**, and **elephants** and honor them in festivals and ceremonies.

HUMANS ARE MAMMALS, TOO

Humans belong to the group of mammals called **primates**, which includes **monkeys** and **apes**. We are similar to our primate relatives in many ways!

Like humans, **monkeys** and **apes** have hands and use them to grip, hold, throw, and pick up things. **Chimps** poke sticks into termite mounds, then pull them out to lick the bugs off the stick.

MAMMALS IN DANGER

Mammals are an essential part of the natural world, but they are in greater danger than ever before. In modern times, eighty-five species of mammals have already gone **extinct**, and nearly a quarter of all mammal species are now at risk of extinction.

There are possibly fewer than ten **vaquitas** left in the world. These rare river porpoises have died out due to water **pollution** and from getting trapped in fishing nets. It's hoped that the last few can be saved before they, too, go extinct.

No one has seen a wild **scimitar-horned oryx** in its natural desert habitat since 1988. These majestic beasts were hunted for their horns, and now they are kept safe behind fences. Hopefully one day they can be released back into the wild.

Cotton-top tamarins live in the forests of South America, but it is thought that only 2,000 of them still survive there. In the past, they were sold as pets, and their habitat has been destroyed in order to build homes for people instead. Scientists and local people are now working hard to save them.

The shrinking jungles of Sumatra, an island in Southeast Asia, are home to fewer than eighty **rhinos**. Their forests have been cut down to make way for farms, and they are hunted for their horns. The last Sumatran rhinos are now kept safe and protected from hunters.

Human childhood is a time of play and learning. The childhood of an **orangutan** lasts about seven years, and during this time the mother cares for her youngster and teaches it how to find the best fruits to eat.

Primates are experts at communicating. They use sounds to talk, but they also use their faces to express how they are feeling. **Chimps** pout and whimper when they are feeling sad, and when they are happy, they make a special smile, with their lower teeth showing.